Questo notebook appartiene a :

....

....

....

....

....

www.ingramcontent.com/pod-product-compliance
Lightning Source LLC
Chambersburg PA
CBHW071449130726
47997CB00006B/2289
* 9 7 9 8 6 0 7 7 7 2 8 8 8 *